HILLARY CLINTON launched her presidential campaign in spring 2015 by venturing from New York to Iowa to rail against income inequality and to propose new spending programs and higher taxes on the wealthy as remedies for it. She reemphasized these dual themes of inequality and redistribution in the "relaunch" of her campaign in June 2015 and in the occasional campaign speeches she delivered over the course of the summer. Clinton's campaign strategy has been interpreted as a concession to influential progressive spokesmen like Senators Elizabeth Warren and Bernie Sanders, who have loudly pressed these redistributionist themes for several years, in response to the financial meltdown in 2008 and out of a long-standing wish to reverse the "Reagan Revolution" of the 1980s. In view of Clinton's embrace of the progressive agenda, there can be little doubt that inequality, higher taxes, and proposals for new spending programs will be central themes in the Democratic presidential campaign in 2

While voters are worried about inequality, they are far more skeptical of the capacity of the government to do anything about it without making matters worse for everyone.

The intellectual case for redistribution has been outlined in impressive detail in recent years by a phalanx of progressive economists – including Thomas Piketty, Joseph Stiglitz, and *New York Times* opinion columnist Paul Krugman – who have called for redistributive tax and spending policies to address the challenge of the growth of inequalities in income and wealth. Piketty's best-selling book, *Capital in the Twenty-First Century* (2014), made a case for raising the top marginal tax rate in the United States from 39.6 percent (where it stands today) to 80 percent or more (where it was during the 1940s and 1950s), and then relying upon the U.S. government to redistribute those funds from the wealthy to households in greater need of them. Nobel Laureate Robert Solow of MIT put the matter bluntly in a 2014 exchange with Harvard's Gregory Mankiw, saying that he is in favor of dealing with inequality by "taking a dollar from a random rich person and giving it to a random poor person," presumably with the federal government acting as the middleman to implement the transaction.

Public-opinion polls over the years have consistently shown that voters overwhelmingly reject programs of redistribution in favor of policies designed to promote overall economic growth and job creation. More-recent polls suggest that while voters are increasingly concerned about inequality and question the high salaries paid to executives and bankers, they nevertheless reject redistributive remedies like higher taxes on the wealthy. According to those studies, voters do not support redistributive policies because they do not believe the government is capable of implementing them in effective ways. While voters are worried about inequality, they are far more skeptical of the capacity of the government to do anything about it without making matters worse for everyone.

Here, as is often the case, there is more wisdom in the public's outlook than in the campaign speeches of Democratic presidential candidates and in the books and opinion columns of progressive economists. Leaving aside the morality of redistribution, the progressive case is based upon a significant fallacy: it assumes that the U.S. government is actually capable of redistributing income from the wealthy to the poor. For reasons of policy, tradition, and institutional design, this is not the case. Whatever one may think of inequality, redistributive fiscal policies are unlikely to do much to reduce it, a point that the voters seem instinctively to understand.

*   *   *

One need only look at the effects of federal tax and spending policies over the past 3½ decades to see that this is so. The chart on page 7, based upon data compiled by the Congressional Budget Office (CBO), displays the national shares of before- and after-tax income for the top 1 percent and 10 percent of the income distribution from 1979 to 2011, along with the same figures for the bottom quintile of the distribution. For purposes of this study, the CBO defined *income* as market income plus government transfers, including cash payments and the value of in-kind services and payments, such as health care (Medicare and Medicaid) and food stamps. The chart thus represents a comprehensive portrait of the degree to which federal tax and spending policies redistribute income from the wealthiest to the poorest groups, and to households in between.

The chart illustrates two broad points. First, the wealthiest groups gradually increased their share of national income (both in pre-

and after-tax and transfer income) over this 30-plus-year period; and second, federal tax and spending policies had little effect on the overall distribution of income.

Across this period, the top 1 percent of the income distribution nearly doubled their share of (pretax) national income, from about 9 percent in 1979 to more than 18 percent in 2007 and 2008, before it fell back after the financial crisis, to 15 percent in 2010 and 2011. (Some studies suggest that by 2014, it was back up to 18 percent.) Meanwhile, the top 10 percent of the income distribution increased their share by a third, from about 30 percent in 1979 to 40 percent in 2007 and 2008, before it fell to 37 percent in 2011. This was a secular trend in the distribution of national income that persisted throughout different presidential administrations and tax regimes. The path was smoothly upward for both income groups across the period, with temporary peaks and troughs corresponding with business-cycle rallies and recessions. Economists have offered different

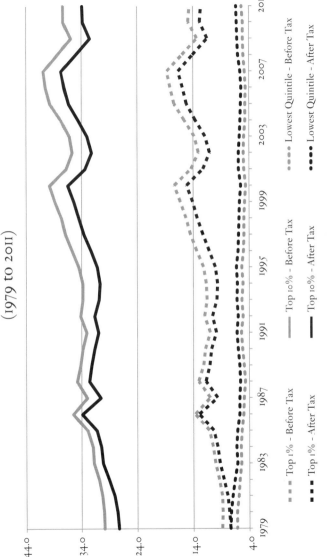

Share of Before- & After-Tax Income
(1979 to 2011)

PERCENT

Source: Congressional Budget Office, "Distribution of Household Income and Federal Taxes, 2011"
(November 12, 2014); https://www.cbo.gov/publication/49440#title1

- - - Top 1% - Before Tax
——— Top 1% - After Tax

——— Top 10% - Before Tax
——— Top 10% - After Tax

• • • Lowest Quintile - Before Tax
••• Lowest Quintile - After Tax

theories to explain the trend, though most agree that the causes lie in several overlapping factors, including globalization, technological change, record stock-market gains, and increasing premiums paid to highly educated workers.

Many will be surprised to learn that the federal fiscal system – taxes and spending – does not do more to reduce inequalities in income that arise from the free-market system. After all, the progressive income tax was designed to redistribute income by placing heavier burdens on the wealthy, and many federal spending programs were crafted specifically to assist lower-income households. Yet there are perfectly obvious reasons, on both the tax and spending sides, as to why redistribution does not succeed in the American system – and probably cannot be made to succeed.

*   *   *

The income tax yields revenues to the government through two main sources: progressive taxes on ordinary income (salaries and wages) and taxes on capital gains, with the latter taxed at somewhat lower rates to encourage investment. For most of this period, taxes on capital gains have yielded less than 10 percent of total income taxes and about 4 percent of total federal revenues. In terms of the income tax, most of the action is in taxes on ordinary income.

The highest marginal income tax rate oscillated up and down from 1979 to 2011. In 1979 during the Carter presidency, it was 70 percent, then it fell to 50 percent and to 28 percent in the Reagan/Bush years. It then rose to 39.6 percent in the 1990s under the Clinton presidency and fell again to 35 percent from 2003 to 2010. (It is now back up to 39.6 percent.) The highest rate on capital gains moved within a narrower band, beginning at 28 percent in 1979 and falling as low as 15 percent from 2005 to 2011. (The top rate is currently 23.5 percent.)

Over this period, regardless of the tax rates, the top 1 percent of the income distribution lost 1 percent to 2 percent of their income share due to taxes. In 1980, that group claimed 9 percent of before-tax income and 8 percent of after-tax income; in 1990 the figures were 12 percent and 11 percent; and in 2010, 15 percent and 13 percent. The top 10 percent of the income distribution generally lost 2 percent to 4 percent of their income share due to taxes, probably because those households take a greater share of their income (compared with the 1 percent) in salaries rather than in capital gains. At the other end, the poorest quintiles gained almost nothing (about 1 percent on average) in income shares due to cash and in-kind transfers from the government. In 2011, for example, the poorest 20 percent of households received 5 percent of (pretax) national income and 6 percent of after-tax income. That pattern was stable and consistent throughout the period.

Many in the redistribution camp attribute this pattern to a lack of progressivity in the U.S. income tax system, an explanation that overlooks the fact that income taxes in the

U.S. are at least as progressive as those in many other developed countries. The highest marginal rate in the U.S. was 35 percent from 2003 to 2012 and today is 39.6 percent for top earners, a rate not far out of line with those of America's chief competitors, including Germany, France, the United Kingdom, and Japan, where the highest marginal rates range between 40 percent and 46 percent.

A 2008 study published by the Organisation for Economic Co-operation and Development (OECD) found that the U.S. had the

---

It would be difficult to make the U.S. income tax system more progressive than it already is in terms of the share of the tax burden carried by the wealthiest households.

---

most progressive income tax system among all 24 OECD countries, measured in terms of the share of the tax burden paid by the wealthiest households. According to the Congressional Budget Office, the top 1 percent of earners paid 39 percent of the personal income taxes in 2010 (while claiming 15 percent of before-tax income), compared with 17 percent in 1980 and 24 percent in 1990. According to the same study, the top 20 percent of earners paid 93 percent of federal income taxes in 2010 while claiming just 52 percent of before-tax income. Meanwhile, the bottom 40 percent of the income distribution paid zero net income taxes. For all practical purposes, those in the highest brackets already bear the overwhelming burden of federal income tax, while those below the median income have been taken out of the income tax system altogether. It would be difficult to make the U.S. income tax system more progressive than it already is in terms of the share of the tax burden carried by the wealthiest households.

*   *   *

There is a more basic reason the tax system does not do more to redistribute income: the progressive income tax is not the primary source of revenue for the U.S. government. In 2010, the federal government raised $2.144 trillion in taxes, with just 42 percent coming from the individual income tax, 40 percent from payroll taxes, 9 percent from corporate taxes, and the rest from a mix of estate and excise taxes. In 2014, due to the economic recovery, the figures had shifted to 46 percent for income taxes and 34 percent for payroll taxes. Since the early 1950s, the national government has consistently relied upon the income tax for 40 percent to 50 percent of its revenues, with precise proportions varying from year to year due to economic conditions. For several generations, progressive reformers have looked to the income tax as the instrument through which they aimed to take resources from the rich and deliver them to the poor. In reality – in the United States, at least – the income tax is not a sufficiently large revenue source for the national government to do the job that the redistributionists want it to do.

During the New Deal era, the United States chose to fund its program of old-age pensions (Social Security) through payroll taxes on employees and employers rather than from general income tax revenues. In adopting this approach, the U.S. followed a precedent established by Germany in the 1880s, when that country established a system of old-age support funded by payroll taxes. President Roosevelt insisted on the payroll tax because he felt the program would be insulated from congressional meddling if it had its own dedicated funding stream. He also feared that Congress would add unaffordable future benefits if the program received its funding from general revenues. The payroll tax also allowed FDR to cast Social Security as an insurance program that provided workers with guaranteed rights to benefits in return for their lifetime contributions. When President Johnson and Congress expanded the program in 1965 to provide medical care for seniors, they chose to fund it with an additional payroll tax. Today, Social Security and Medicare are the two most expensive domestic programs funded by the federal government – and they are paid for by pay-roll taxes.

As a result of the passage of Medicare and expansions in Social Security benefits, payroll taxes as a share of federal revenues doubled during the 1960s and 1970s, from 16 percent of revenues in 1960 to well over 30 percent by the late 1970s. Payroll taxes fall more heavily upon working- and middle-class incomes, which come from wages and salaries, than upon the wealthy, whose incomes come dis-proportionately from capital gains and whose salaries far exceed the maximum earnings subject to those taxes. In 2010, the wealthiest 1 percent paid just 4 percent of payroll taxes (compared with 39 percent of income taxes), and the top quintile of earners paid 45 percent of payroll taxes (compared with 93 percent of income taxes), while the middle quintile of earners paid 15 percent of all payroll taxes (and just 3 percent of income taxes). The payroll tax has progressive features, in that the wealthy still carry a heavier share than the poor, but it is far less progressive than the income tax. And in terms of the federal tax system as a whole, the more widely shared burdens of the payroll tax tend to offset or mitigate the progressive effects of the income tax.

When those two revenue streams – income and payroll taxes – are added together, the federal tax system appears substantially less progressive than when assessed solely in terms of income taxes. In 2010 (according to CBO data), the top 1 percent of the income distribution paid 24 percent of total taxes, compared with 39 percent of individual income taxes, and earned 15 percent of the (pretax) national income. The top 20 percent of the income distribution paid 69 percent of total taxes, compared with 93 percent of income taxes, and earned 52 percent of the national income. Meanwhile, the middle quintile of household incomes paid 9 percent of total taxes but just 3 percent of individual income taxes, while claiming 14 percent of the national income. The federal tax system remains modestly progressive when the two taxes are added together, because the wealthier households still pay a larger share of total taxes than they claim in total national income. Nevertheless, the federal government's reliance on payroll taxes to fund generous entitlement programs mitigates the progressivity of the income tax.

This factor makes it exceedingly difficult for the government to redistribute income in any substantial way through the federal tax system. The payroll tax as a means of funding entitlements is embedded financially and politically into the federal system. It would be difficult from a political point of view to untangle and redesign that system of funding, given the current divisions between the two political parties. It would also be unwise for a host of reasons – most of them outlined by President Roosevelt in the 1930s – to attempt

---

The income tax is not a sufficiently large revenue source for the national government to do the job that the redistributionists want it to do.

---

a switch to general revenues to pay for those expensive and politically popular programs, because it would tempt Congress to add future benefits without regard to costs. Whatever one may think of them, payroll taxes are not going to disappear as sources of revenue for Social Security and Medicare.

That leaves redistributionists with the option of raising income tax rates on "the rich" – defined as the top 1 percent of the income distribution – but there is not enough money available by that route to make much of a difference to the other 99 percent of the population, or to those in the bottom half of the income distribution. An increase in the top marginal tax rate from 39.6 percent to, say, 50 percent might have yielded about $100 billion in additional revenue in 2010, assuming no corresponding changes in tax and income strategies on the part of wealthy households and no negative effects on investment and economic growth (all risky assumptions). That is real money, to be sure, but it represented only about 0.5 percent of GDP (using 2010 figures) and less than 3 percent of total federal spending, not enough to permit much in the way of redistribution to the roughly 60 million households in the bottom half of the income scale. This also assumes that federal expenditures actually redistribute income from the rich to the poor or to those in between, which is most definitely not the case.

*   *   *

Turning to the spending side of fiscal policy, we encounter a somewhat murkier situation because of the sheer number and complexity of federal spending programs. Nevertheless, the conclusion is much the same as on the tax side: the overall flow of federal spending does little to alter shares of national income between the top and bottom of the income scale. In fact, federal expenditures, when taken as a whole, fail to redistribute income from the rich to the poor and instead allocate it upward to the top 20 percent or 30 percent of the income distribution. While we might raise taxes on the wealthy, it does not follow that those revenues would flow to those near or below the poverty line.

This generalization holds despite the fact that the federal government spends roughly half of its $3.5 trillion annual budget on a multitude of programs designed to assist the elderly, the disabled, the poor, and the near poor. The House of Representatives Budget Committee estimated in 2012 that the federal government spent nearly $800 billion on

92 antipoverty programs that provided cash assistance, medical care, housing assistance, food stamps, and tax credits for the poor and near poor. The number of people drawing benefits from antipoverty programs has more than doubled since the 1980s, from 42 million in 1983 to 108 million in 2011. The redistributive effects of these programs are limited, however, because most funds are spent on services to assist the poor, and only a small fraction of these expenditures is distributed in the form of cash or income. Most of the money, in short, goes to providers of services and not to poor or near-poor households.

This is an important feature of the American welfare state as it has evolved over the decades: it is organized to assist the poor and to alleviate the conditions of poverty, but not to redistribute income from the wealthy to the poor. The American welfare state mostly provides in-kind services and benefits to the poor as opposed to cash income, with the result that most of the actual money spent on poverty goes to households that are far from poor.

Former Senator Daniel Patrick Moynihan once tartly described this as "feeding the sparrows by feeding the horses" – in other words, paying middle-class and upper-middle-class providers to deliver services to the poor. (Moynihan was in favor of delivering incomes rather than services to the poor.)

The federal government's reliance on payroll taxes to fund generous entitlement programs mitigates the progressivity of the income tax.

The U.S. welfare state evolved in the direction of services rather than incomes in part because the American people have long viewed poverty as a condition to be overcome rather than one to be subsidized with cash. Many also believe that the poor would squander or misspend cash payments and so are better off receiving services and in-kind benefits like food stamps, health care, and tuition assistance. For the most part, then, Americans have erected an array of "safety net" programs designed to help people who are temporarily in need move out of poverty or prevent them from falling into destitution. With regard to providing aid to the poor, then, Americans have built a social-service state but not a redistribution state.

* * *

Social Security is the only substantial federal program that transfers money from one group to another, in this case from workers and employers paying payroll taxes to retirees collecting benefits. It is by far the largest of all federal programs and claimed $850 billion, or 24 percent of the federal budget, in 2014. It is paid for by a payroll tax split equally between employees and employers. As of 2014, about 59 million Americans were collecting benefits under Social Security, with an average benefit of $1,260 per month.

Social Security has a progressive benefit formula, and it contains a feature (Supplemental Security Income) that provides cash benefits to elderly, blind, or disabled people with incomes below the poverty line. Nevertheless, in spite of those features, it was designed and still functions to provide income for retirees, not to redistribute income from the wealthy to the poor. Because retirees have paid into the system via payroll taxes, Social Security (like Medicare) is not means-tested. Everyone who has paid in is eligible to receive benefits, regardless of wealth or income. The system operates on a pay-as-you-go basis such that incomes for current retirees are funded by taxes on current workers and employers.

The National Bureau of Economic Research (NBER), in a series of studies on the redistributive aspects of Social Security, concluded that the program transfers income in various complex ways (for example, from those with short life expectancies to those with longer ones) but over the long run does not transfer it from the rich to the poor. One NBER study by Julia Lynn Coronado, Don Fullerton, and Thomas Glass bluntly concluded that "Social Security does not redistribute from people who are rich over their lifetime to those who are poor. In fact, it may even be slightly regressive." This is partly because wealthier recipients tend to live longer than others and partly because they are more likely to have nonworking spouses who are also eligible to collect benefits.

Medicare and Medicaid, two other expensive programs that together claim nearly 25 percent of the federal budget, provide important health care services to the elderly and the poor but no actual income. Medicare (like Social Security) is funded through payroll taxes and Medicaid through a roughly 60/40 mix of federal and state taxes. There are currently about 56 million elderly Americans enrolled in Medicare and about 71 million low-income Americans enrolled in Medicaid and its affiliated program, the Children's Health Insurance Program (CHIP). There are an additional 9 million people enrolled in Women, Infants, and Children (WIC), a separate program set up to deliver food and nutritional assistance to pregnant women and mothers of young children in families with incomes below or slightly above the poverty line. Enrollment in all these programs is growing rapidly because of the aging of the population (Medicare) and the expansion of Medicaid under the Affordable Care Act. Medicaid is now the most rapidly growing item in state budgets across the country.

The flow of money through these health care programs – more than $850 billion in federal funds in 2014 (plus another $180 billion in state funds for Medicaid) – goes mainly to hospitals, nursing homes, pharmaceutical companies, doctors, insurance companies, and health-maintenance organizations. These two programs underwrite more than 60 percent of expenditures on nursing homes in the United States and more than 30 percent of national expenditures on hospital care. Both programs have been plagued by fraud and corruption since their origins in 1965 because some doctors, nursing-home entrepreneurs, and other providers have sought to game the system for financial advantage – and in many cases have succeeded all too well. No one has ever attempted a study of the redistributive aspects of the flow of funds from Medicare and Medicaid, but one surmises from the nature of these payments (to insurance companies, nursing homes, and doctors, for example) that most of the money goes to those in the upper reaches of the income distribution.

*   *   *

The federal government provides cash assistance to the poor and near poor through two programs: (1) Temporary Assistance to Needy Families (TANF, popularly known as welfare), which currently provides cash benefits to about 4.5 million households at a cost of $17 billion per year to the federal government and about $14 billion (in 2014) to various state governments; and (2) Supplemental Security Income, which provides cash benefits to the disabled poor (8.5 million households) at a cost of about $50 billion per year to the federal government. These numbers work out to about $7,000 (on average) per year per household under TANF and $6,000 per year per household under SSI, in each case, about half of the average benefit under Social Security.

The cash transfers under TANF may be regarded as redistributions because they are paid for out of general income tax revenues, at least at the federal level, and the funds go exclusively to poor households. The funds paid out under SSI are collected via Social Security payroll taxes and thus, for reasons outlined above, cannot be judged as redistributions from the wealthy to the poor. SSI

> *With regard to providing aid to the poor, Americans have built a social-service state but not a redistribution state.*

expenditures have increased rapidly in recent years as TANF expenditures have fallen, in part because (as the House Budget Committee Report suggests) some states have moved able-bodied welfare recipients to SSI, where they are supported exclusively by federal funds. Lower-income working families are also eligible to receive rebates on payroll taxes through the Earned Income Tax Credit (EITC). The House Budget Committee estimated that 28 million taxpayers took advantage of this program in 2011, at an estimated cost of $60 billion to the federal government in rebated taxes. (The average family with children received $2,900 in tax rebates.)

The poor are eligible to receive a bevy of in-kind benefits under Medicaid, the Supplemental Nutrition Assistance Program (SNAP, formerly known as food stamps), rental assistance, college scholarships, energy subsidies, job training, and other programs too numerous to list. Next to Medicaid, SNAP is the most expensive and far-reaching of these programs. It provided in-kind food subsidies to some 47 million people in 2014, at a cost of $74 billion to the federal government (about $16 billion of which went to administration). A qualifying individual could receive (in 2014) a maximum benefit of $194 per month, and a family of four could receive up to $650 per month. The federal government pays out these benefits on the first of each month by reloading a government-issued credit card to be used solely for purchases of food and beverages at supermarkets and convenience stores. SNAP comes close to providing a cash benefit, since recipients can use their cards to purchase a wide range of items at retail stores, and, indeed, some exchange their cards for cash in an underground market. SNAP is supported in Congress by influential lobbying groups, including agricultural interests and food manufacturers, which supply the food distributed through the program; and major retail chains, where recipients redeem their benefits.

Of the $800 billion spent on poverty programs in 2012 (as listed in the House Budget Committee Report), it appears that less than $150 billion, or about 18 percent of the total, was distributed in cash income, if we include as a cash benefit the tax rebate under the EITC. The rest of the funds were spent on services and in-kind benefits, with the money paid to providers of various kinds, most of whom have incomes well above the poverty line. It is worth noting that when President Obama sought to build out the welfare state, he did so mainly by expanding in-kind benefit programs, particularly Medicaid and SNAP.

With respect to the recipients of federal

transfers, the CBO study reveals a surprising fact: households in the bottom quintile of the income distribution receive less in federal payments than those in the higher-income quintiles. According to that study, households in the bottom quintile of the income distribution (below $24,000 in income per year) received on average $8,600 in cash and in-kind transfers; households in the middle quintile about $16,000 in such transfers; and households in the highest quintile about $11,000. Even households in the top 1 percent of the distribution received more in dollar transfers than those in the bottom quintile. The wealthier households received those transfers overwhelmingly through Social Security and Medicare; the poorer households from a roughly equal mix of Social Security, Medicare, Medicaid, TANF (cash welfare), and SNAP (food stamps). The federal transfer system may move income around and through the economy, but it does not redistribute it from the rich to the poor or near poor.

* * *

The above programs accounted for more than 60 percent of all federal spending in 2014. Most of the remainder of the $3.5 trillion in federal expenditures was allocated to budget items whose purposes are unrelated to redistribution – including defense, medical research, transportation, agricultural subsidies, veterans' benefits, small-business loans, and interest on the national debt. The evidence we have suggests that the bulk of these funds flow in the direction of households well above the median national income.

American Transparency, a research organization that posts government payments online, discovered that *Fortune* 100 companies receive more than $100 billion per year in federal contracts and subsidies, much of it through the defense, aerospace, and transportation budgets. The same organization found that the largest farm subsidies flow into wealthy urban zip codes in New York City, Beverly Hills, Palm Beach, Miami Beach, and Sea Island, Ga. Wealthy investors are said to have purchased farmland in order to claim the agricultural subsidies attached to it.

A parallel analysis of other federal spending programs would reveal much the same pattern. Interest payments on the national debt – roughly $230 billion in 2014 – flow to foreign governments, pension funds, mutual

---

The federal transfer system may move income around and through the economy, but it does not redistribute it from the rich to the poor or near poor.

---

funds, and individual investors, but very little of it goes back to households at the bottom or the lower half of the income scale. For this reason, deficit spending (now the norm in Washington, D.C.) is one of the most regressive of all federal policies.

An impressive amount of federal spending

flows to charitable and not-for-profit organizations that provide their employees and executives with generous salaries and benefits. The publication *Giving USA*, which tracks charitable spending, reports that the government now supplies one-third of all funds raised by not-for-profit organizations. According to a study by the National Science Foundation, major research universities received federal grants and contracts totaling $40 billion in 2011. Johns Hopkins led the pack with $1.9 billion, followed by the University of Washington ($949 million), the University of Michigan ($820 million), and the University of Pennsylvania ($707 million). If one leaves aside the large sums allocated to these institutions, the nonprofit sector still received $215 billion in federal grants and contracts in 2010, more than 6 percent of total federal spending.

*   *   *

It is well known in Washington that the people and groups that lobby for federal programs are generally those who receive the salaries and income, rather than those who get the services. They – as Moynihan observed decades ago – are the direct beneficiaries of most of these programs, and they have the strongest interest in keeping them going as they are. The nation's capital is home to countless trade associations; companies seeking government contracts; hospital and medical associations lobbying for Medicare and Medicaid expenditures; agricultural groups; college and university lobbyists; and advocacy organizations for the environment, the elderly, and the poor, all of them seeking a share of federal grants and contracts or some form of subsidy or tax break.

This is the reason five of the seven wealthiest counties in the nation border on Washington, D.C., and is also why the average income for the District of Columbia's top 5 percent of households exceeds $500,000, the highest among major American cities. Washington is among the nation's most unequal cities as measured by the income gap between the wealthy and everyone else.

Those wealthy individuals did not descend upon the nation's capital in order to redistribute income to the poor but rather to secure some benefit to their institutions, industries, and, incidentally, to themselves. They understand a basic principle that has so far eluded progressives and redistributionists: the federal government is an effective engine for dispensing patronage, encouraging rent seeking, and circulating money to important voting blocs and well-connected constituencies – but not for the redistribution of income.

This point also provides perspective on the "makers vs. takers" theme that one often hears in Republican criticisms of federal-transfer programs. In fact, the distinction between makers and takers is not so easy to establish. The roster of the so-called takers does not consist exclusively of poor people and deadbeats who refuse to work or pay taxes (though there is some of this). Many of the takers are elderly beneficiaries of Social Security and Medicare, middle-class professionals who provide public services of one

> *The people and groups that lobby for federal programs are generally those that receive the salaries and income, rather than those who get the services.*

kind or another, and financially comfortable recipients of government grants and contracts. Many of the takers, in short, are middle- and upper-middle-class voters, which is one reason efforts to scale back the government are met with so much resistance. Aaron Director, the late economist at the University of Chicago, maintained decades ago that government programs are structured and paid for primarily to satisfy middle-class voters. Despite the evolution of the American welfare state in recent decades, his proposition remains valid today.

James Madison wrote in *The Federalist* that

the possession of different degrees and kinds of property is the most durable source of faction under a popularly elected government. Madison especially feared the rise of redistributive politics, under which the poor might seize the reins of government in order to plunder the wealthy by heavy taxes. He and his colleagues introduced various political mechanisms – the intricate system of checks and balances in the Constitution, federalism, and the dispersion of interests across an extended republic – to forestall a division between the rich and poor in America and to deflect political conflict into other channels. While Madison's design did not succeed in holding back the tide of big government in the 20th century, it nevertheless proved robust enough to frustrate the aims of redistributionists by promoting a national establishment that is open to a boundless variety of crisscrossing interests.

The ingrained character of the American state is unlikely to change fundamentally anytime soon, which is why those who worry about inequality should abandon the failed cause of redistribution and turn their attention instead to broad-based economic growth as the only practical remedy for the sagging incomes of too many Americans.

First American edition published in 2015 by Encounter Books,
an activity of Encounter for Culture and Education, Inc.,
a nonprofit, tax exempt corporation.
Encounter Books website address: www.encounterbooks.com

Manufactured in the United States and printed on
acid-free paper. The paper used in this publication meets
the minimum requirements of ANSI/NISO Z39.48–1992
(R 1997) (*Permanence of Paper*).

FIRST AMERICAN EDITION

LIBRARY OF CONGRESS CATALOGING-IN-PUBLICATION DATA

Piereson, James.
Why redistribution fails / James Piereson.
pages   cm. — (Encounter broadsides ; 45)
ISBN 978-1-59403-873-0 (pbk. : alk. paper) —
ISBN 978-1-59403-874-7 (ebook)
1. Income distribution—United States. 2. Distributive justice–United
States. 3. Fiscal policy—United States. 4. Taxation—United States.
5. United States—Economic conditions—2009– I. Title.
HC110.I5P54 2016
339.2'2—dc23
2015030502

10 9 8 7 6 5 4 3 2 1

SERIES DESIGN BY CARL W. SCARBROUGH